The Beginning

The Book of B.L.A.C.
Born Leader Accepting Criticsm

ARCARDIO "CARAVEGGIO" HARDEN

Copyright

Forward

God wants you to know what the devil does not want you to see - Caraveggio

Dedication

This book is dedicated to my nephew, Darrell Dashon Perkins, and all the angels God has sent my way; to my brothers Nate and JB - there is a heaven for kings; to all others I lost along my journey - see you all in heaven; to the ones that look up to me - always remember to keep reaching for the stars and never give up because there is a leader inside of you

Caraveggio

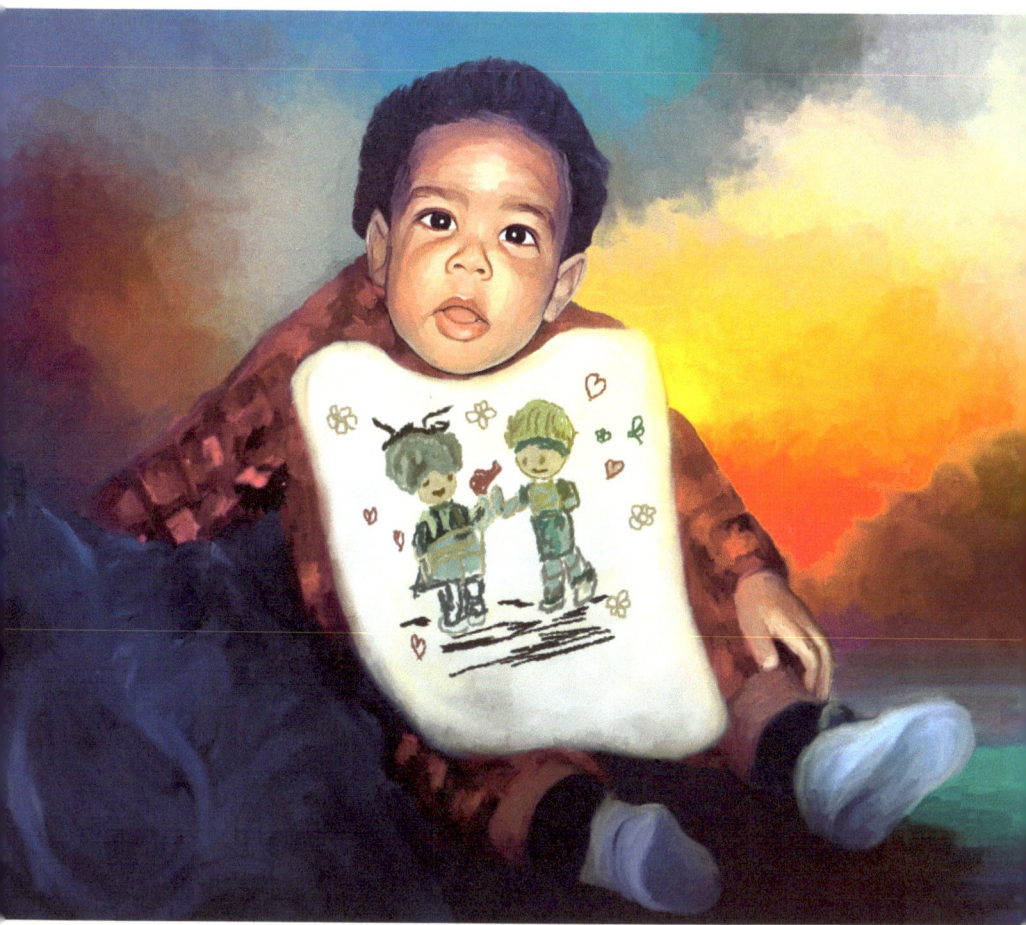

Don't ever think one is stupid because that one could be the greatest man you have ever seen walk this planet earth

Caraveggio

CHAPTER 1

The Meaning

B.L.A.C.

Born Leader Accepting Criticism

The Making of a Man

To those who stood by my side

when I was frustrated ready to die,

I know you said a prayer for me.

Your freedom cry

gave me my wings, so I could touch the sky,

so you wouldn't have to say your last goodbyes.

To those who never understood,

who thought I didn't have a plan,

all that criticism helped raise a real B.L.A.C. man.

Let me break it down so a fetus could understand...

Look into my eyes, you will see pictures of what I've been through -

a lost soul, blinded from the truth,

trapped in this cold world, on a quest for peace,

a cloud over my shoulders from the cruel and deceased.

Damn, man, I need another Kool!

We all know we have to live and learn,

even if it takes a cigarette or weed to burn.

I went from a depression, to asking questions;

to building up my lust, to my confessions.

5 steps to the pool, where I'm baptized,

I kiss my past goodbye,

hoping my prayers reach the sky.

I'm no lesser of a man,

I just hope you understand - the makings of a B.L.A.C. man.

Birth of B.L.A.C.

If I could remember my thoughts from back when I was in my mother's womb, I know my thoughts would be like..."Am I gonna be loved once I get outta here? Will people perceive me well? Will life take its toll on me? Will I fail? Will I be surrounded by good people? Will the world love me? Will I grow to be one of the greatest men who ever walked the planet earth?" Only time will tell.

So far in 2013, since my birth, life has had its ups and downs, roadblocks and traps, but God has been here to pull me out of the fire ever since. With time, I've learned alot. I've met good people and bad people, I've surrounded myself with good positive people, I have found rabbits. I know now if I want to be a billionaire while in my thirties or even before I die, I will have to have a roadmap and a game plan.

It took me a while in order to learn the game. Even when I was in high school I went through alot, but I didn't know the game. I didn't know the game of life. Everybody says had I known what I know now I wouldn't be in this position. Hell, I say that, but at the same time I thank God for putting me through the obstacles that He's put me through. That way, when victory is accomplished I will be more proud of my accomplishments and more thankful for what I've been through in order to get my goals and dreams accomplished.

People love trying to look into your life and trying to figure out who you are or where you've been. To me, people can be the cruelest thing on this planet earth. I think people are so cruel because life is a competition. Every day when you wake up, whether you like it or not, you are in the game of life. If you refuse to play you become a lamb on the streets waiting for a handout. Life is a competition, and it doesn't matter if you are in sports, modeling, school, or whatever, somebody will always want to criticize you or be like you.

Looking back on my life in my younger days, I really have had my share of cruel people in my life that tried to take advantage of me, belittle me, convince me to do things I didn't want to do, and treat me like I was nothing. To them I was the scum of the earth, but with time I grew and became a better person, a better man, a wiser man, a man with a backbone, and a man who wasn't so passive about things. In time I learned that once you let someone get over on you, they will try it for the rest of your life. So I had to learn to nip things in the bud before they even got started, and I learned to do that very well.

3

I think life is so crazy, for the simple fact that when you are in the womb of your mother, you are this precious child that doesn't know anything. When you get out of the womb you still don't know anything. You are taught to be nice and wise and to make smart decisions in life and to treat people with respect. Then as you get older you find out how people really are and how life really works - either you stand up for something, or you stand for nothing; either the next man will respect you, or he will disrespect you. You turn from this angel to this devil in your own right. I'm not talking about a devil like you're sent from hell or you're going to hell. I'm talking about in order to be somebody, in order to be respected and not let people run all over you, you will learn that you can't be an angel all the time. You can be an angel for God, but while you're here on this planet earth people will see your other side. Everybody has two sides to them, nobody wants to be considered a push-over, I mean nobody. In this life you can either stand up for what you believe in, protect what is right to you and yours, or you will die a nobody that always got pushed around until the day you die.

So before I get into my story, my life, my testimony on how I became **B.L.A.C.** (a **B**orn **L**eader **A**ccepting **C**riticism), you need to sit back and think about the pride and the heart within you. Before you start to read my life, you need to make a conscious decision on what you want to do with your life and never judge mine or another's, and, even if you do, I am **B.L.A.C.**, so I can and I will turn whatever negative you come at me with, into a positive.

4

My Story, My Life, My Testimony

From what I understand, I was a mistake, I wasn't even suppose to be here. From what I was told, my sister wanted another sister, not a brother. From what I understand, my mother got bigger, so she stopped eating so she wouldn't get any bigger. But, you know, God knows best because I survived, and I'm still here breathing. I'm alive, and you know, they all grew to love me anyway. Family first; it's all love; to the top we go; respect all, but fear none.

When I was younger I was quiet and withdrawn. I didn't like people then, just about as much as I do now. I knew then that people could be so hateful and so cruel. They can use you and abuse you and not give a fuck. I hung around my sister D alot because I just didn't like the outside world and the people in it. I didn't have any brothers, just two older sisters, so automatically I would just look up to them for guidance and inspiration. I didn't read books back then, I didn't get into them like that. I didn't start reading books until after high school. Once you find out which book is for you and you like it, you will be hooked. Anything that you want to know you can find in books, all you have to do is find out which one is for you. People say they hate to read and they will never read. I look at it like this - you're not going to like every movie or video game or album that comes out, but you take a chance with them, so why not take a chance with a book and increase your knowledge and make your life better and become a better person.

One of the main things I learned from being around my sisters is how to be a gentleman. That's one thing a boy will learn if he is raised around alot of women and that is how to treat a woman. I know for a fact that I got my music but from my sister, Lisa, because she is a music fanatic. She had every single R&B album that came out from Gerald Levert, to Keith Sweat, to Johnny Gill. I didn't get introduced to hip-hop until that one day my sister came in with Tupac's "Me Against the World", and ever since then I was hooked. While she would be buying R&B cd's, I would have her buy me rap cd's. It's funny how I got the money for them now that I think about it. You know, if you didn't get free lunch you had to pay for lunch. Well I would go to school, charge my lunch, and keep the money, and then sometimes my sister would put the other half with it. Now let me tell you, lunch was $1.25, so what I would do sometimes is ask my parents for an extra dollar, that way my money would add up faster.

Life really started moving when I was in middle school. That's when life started changing. I would be called "Prettyboy", and kids would tease me all day. When I didn't eat lunch they would say things like, "Damn, if you don't eat you might die today" or some other shit. I remember being bullied by kids for no reason. I guess because I was quiet and withdrawn and stayed to myself the kids would bully me. People always say what don't kill you only makes you stronger. Well I believe in that with all my heart. As I look back on my life I can actually say I've come a long way. If you can't look back on your life and thank God for what He has put you through, then something is wrong.

I remember being on the basketball team, and I was really good, so you know hotties came in flocks. I know for a fact that most of my teammates hated me and wanted me to fall, and me being young and weak-hearted, I fell and they all laughed at me. I learned that some people in life can't stand to see someone do better than themselves, no matter how good life or people treats them. When things like that started happening to me, I really got withdrawn from people because at that point in my life I didn't know how to handle it, I didn't know how to fight back. One thing bullies don't realize is that once they start messing with weak individuals, eventually those weak individuals grow up.

Most bullies are insecure and have low self-esteem. I remember the girls loved me, like I said, they used to call me "Prettyboy," and I didn't know how to take it. If I knew then what I know now I would have been something like Max Julien. Middle school had its good times and bad times; it taught me a lesson that I will never forget: be careful whom you choose as your friends because friends will be the ones who envy you the most.

Then high school came. If somebody would have said I would go to three different high schools, almost die, starve, watch my grandmother die, watch my other grandmother get rolled out her house in a body bag, and so much more, I would have told them to stop lying and stop wishing so much hate on me and my family. But it was true, it all became a reality, and these events changed my life forever. After I went through all of that I would never be the same. My heart turned cold. I hated people because I didn't trust people. I was sad, lonely, and depressed, and then I just faded to **B.L.A.C.**

I remember as a child that I always wanted to be like my father and play for the same high school team as he did, Brooks High School. Well if you think friends will bring you down, watch your family. Long story short, if you're not careful, your own family will take you out.

I wanted to be the man in football, and I really don't think my family wanted me to be successful because, if they did, things wouldn't have been like that, they would have found a way for me to succeed. But things to me were different. I damn near lost my mind, going from house to house, having to eat over friends' houses because my family wouldn't save me any dinner after football practice. You know, when you're young, you are told that certain people love you. Make sure you have the final decision for yourself.

While all that was going on, I had witnessed my grandmother's passing, and that was the craziest shit I have ever seen - someone pass that you love. You see their eyes roll back in their head, you see their fingers draw up, and when they talk they talk in tongues you can't understand. That really changed how I viewed life in general because if she can go just like that, I can too. So that's why I try to live life like there is no tomorrow.

I believe I witnessed that death right before I moved to Killen, right after my freshman year in high school. During my sophomore and junior years in high school, my other grandmother died, and when we went to her house, they were bringing her out in a body bag. So to me, time and the appreciation of the present mean everything because you just don't know when somebody is going to go.

Besides the way my family tried to starve me out and had me going from house to house, I didn't know where I was going to sleep or eat. It really fucked me up mentally. But I forgive them, and I will never hold a grudge towards my family because they can go just like everybody else, and I know they are smart enough to live and learn and redeem themselves in the future.

By the time I was a senior in high school, I had to move back to Florence, where I didn't want to go and felt people there didn't love me. So I felt uncomfortable going back to Florence, especially after leaving Brooks, a place where I thought my goals and dreams would all come true. I thought people were going to laugh at me and look at me as a failure. People were already talking like I wasn't going to graduate high school. I remember my math teacher saying that if I moved to Florence, I wasn't going to make it out of high school. I had made up my mind, I was going to prove them wrong.

When I finally arrived there, I was excited, depressed, and everything else, but I knew in my heart that I didn't care about what people thought about me because I was determined to make it out of high school. I ended up having to pass two math classes just to graduate, along with all the graduation exams. I did just that - I graduated and walked with my head high and proud across the stage, but most of all I came up with the name **B.L.A.C.**, meaning **B**orn **L**eader **A**ccepting **C**riticism.

One day at the lunch table, I was thinking of something different to put on my senior shirt, something that was meaningful and powerful and described me as a person. At that time in my life, **B.L.A.C.** meant one day I would change the world, and I still believe in that to this day. But little did I know that there is more to life than just misery, suffering, and pain. I had to learn that in order to win in life you have to have a roadmap in order to get the attention of people - the ones who didn't like me or hate me now, the ones who starved me, the ones who have tried to make me suffer. I had no choice but to kill them with my success, to build my own empire from scratch, with soldiers, brick by brick, my striving to be a GOD KING in my own right, in my own empire, with my GOD QUEEN by my side.

You see, I'm still alive, even in 2016. God has His hands on me and has molded me into the man I am suppose to be and is still molding the definition of the leader I am suppose to be. I believe nobody on this planet earth can stop me, only God. Yea, I can get shot, stabbed, or whatever, but you know what, by the time you read this book, my seeds will be planted, and my dreams and I will live forever. Lord forgive them for what they don't know.

8

Letter to Iceberg Slim

I read your book, it had me hooked,

especially that chapter about pepper;

I was in a similar situation, it made me feel better

that I could relate to your situation.

Had I known what I know now,

I would've went for a fresh turnout,

but instead I chose a bitch with game,

who was on the verge of burnout.

Man, what a young naive nigga I was, Slim:

you can turn a good girl bad,

but not a bad girl good, huh?

There's a difference between a woman and a bitch,

and now it's understood,

it's a thin line between a woman and a bitch that the boy in me never understood.

It's like the ying and the yang,

see now it all meshes since in life we all grow

and go through alot of growing pains,

but it only made me stronger,

it only made me a better man.

You know, I had to learn

either you a pimp or a ho; either you a boy or a man;

either you have a backbone, or you don't;

either you have balls, or you don't.

So either pimp or be pimped was something I had to understand;

I learned from you, Slim, and now I'm a changed man.

I learned from Ken Ivy and American Pimp too,

but nobody inspires me more to be a pimp at life, more than you.

You opened my eyes, Slim,

you gave me alot of game, you gave me hope,

and for that I take my hat off to you, man.

It's not just about pimpin a bitch,

or controlling a bitch's mind,

it's about taking on life, with the right frame of mind.

So thanks for the game, Slim, you change my life,

and for that, Slim, I know I owe you my life.

You're a piece of my heart, you're imbedded in my soul,

and not another bitch will ever get close to me

to use me, may God take my soul.

CHAPTER 2

RULE 1
Success starts at home

No Glorification

Never will I glorify a bitch.

I will never speak of your name,

the world will never know you,

the world will never know your name.

If it was up to me

you wouldn't exist,

but instead I leave it to God,

so therefore you will never exist;

you will never make it that far, you see.

I can do alot of things to you

that would only hurt me,

so I leave it up to God

Cause He knows how deep you hurt me.

You see, there's nothing I can do to you

that God can do better,

so I leave it in His hands

because I know He'll make me feel better.

As long as I stay away and pray

and continue to move forward

and mind my business and continue to move forward,

I will surpass you with ease

whether I'm dead or livin.

You see, you will be locally known,

I will be internationally known,

and that's a big difference.

You love the fame and attention,

I just want to live wealthy

and thank God for me livin.

I know I will go far,

even through all this pain,

and I will put it on my life

I will never mention your name,

but you know who you are, bitch!

Rule 1: Success Starts at Home

If you're not happy at home, move out and start a new life. Alot of people stay in bad relationships and unfit homes, thinking that's all God has planned for them, and that's the end of the line for them. When in reality, they're slowly killing themselves, trust me I know. I feel you can only be blessed if God sees progress, and you can only see success if you move forward. Peace of mind means alot. Why come home to hell, when home is suppose to be heaven; why go home to an argument or to someone who doesn't love you, when you can do better by yourself and love yourself? Nobody, and I mean nobody, can love you more than you love yourself, only God. Why would you want to wake up to an argument, go to sleep with an argument, and live the rest of your life in hell? Life is all in what you make it - it can be hell on earth, or it can be heaven on earth.

First things first, everybody needs peace of mind. How can you dream without peace of mind, how can you think without peace of mind? Alot of people grow old early because of misery and stress. Have you ever seen somebody that's young but looks old? Ask them about their home life, and I bet you they will tell you a miserable story or that they are very unhappy or lie, but we all know the truth. Life is for the living, not the dead, so live and live happily. People say they want to be successful, but what is success without peace of mind? People say they want to be successful, but what is success without drive and ambition? You can have so much going on at home that when it comes to life and achieving your goals and dreams you are to exhausted to do so.

Have you ever sat down at home, turned off the lights, television, or radio, nobody's home, and meditated and thought about what you want to do with your life? Instead of hanging out every night doing things that will get you nowhere in life, try sitting down one day and figuring out what you want to do with your life.

Have you ever met someone who hates their job, complains about their job, or tries to make a career out of minimum wage jobs? Do you think those people ever sat down and thought about what they really wanted out of life and tried to put the same effort into their goals and dreams? I'll let you be the judge. Those are the same people who say they are about to retire. Retire to what? What is so happy about sitting at home with nothing, and how can you retire from a minimum wage job? My point is this - figure out what you want to do with your life so you can better your life. I love people, don't get me wrong, but I feel we as one have to be smarter in making decisions about life, that way, at an early age we can enjoy our vacations and do it while we're young because you only live young once.

If you do have a good woman at home, make sure you take care of home. That's very important in a relationship and having peace of mind where you lay your head at night. If you have a good woman make sure you first protect her from harm, lover her until the end of time, and cherish every moment with her because tomorrow is never promised. You can have all the goals and dreams in the world, but what is a dream without love? Of course you can love yourself, and God loves you, but we all know there's nothing like a woman's heart, other than your mother's. We all know there are stars out there that have all the money in the world and still aren't happy because they have nobody to share it with. So what's a dream without love? Nothing.

There are people out there with alot of money, who end up depressed and committing suicide because of a lack of love. I say, wake up and realize that money can't give you good advice on life that can get you through trials and tribulations. Money can't be your love. You can have all the ideas in the world, but what's a good idea if you don't have anybody to share them with? What's a good secret if you have nobody to trust and tell it to? At the end of the day, I say, what's a king without a queen, and what's a queen without a king? Nothing.

So what's success without love? I say, success starts at home, and of course you can achieve success by yourself, for yourself, and be selfish, but at the end of the day nobody wants to be alone. I think even God wants to be loved by someone. You can have all the success in the world, but what's success without love? Life is about moving forward, and we all go through things in life that we have to forgive ourselves for or it will eventually take a toll on us. Nobody is perfect, and at the end of the day we are all human and we all make mistakes. It's up to us to fix them and move forward with our lives. If you have trouble forgiving yourself, pray about it, and God will show you the way because God makes all things better. God is a forgiving God, and He forgives by all means. At the end of the day, God didn't create us perfect, nobody is perfect, life is a game, play to win, and with god on your side you will win. Always keep a clear head to think things through and to have a clear vision to see things through.

So just remember, success starts at home, love the one you're with, and home is where the heart is.

CHAPTER 3

RULE 2

Life is a Game to be Played

Life is a Game to be Played

In life there are rules

rules just like an ordinary game.

a game full of happiness, misery, and pain.

If you plan, plot, strategize

your dreams will stay alive,

but if not your dreams will slowly die.

There will be roadblocks, by crooked cops,

by crooked people, who are so evil,

but it's up to you to surround yourself with good people.

You only live once, you never live twice,

so live life to the fullest

and cherish every second of your life.

Make the best of the bad

and take the bad with the good,

as long as you're progressing, it's still all good.

Run circles around enemies and watch them fall,

while your kingdom stands, and you forever stand tall.

Put your faith in God, put your life in God's hands

Cause you and me both know He already knows your plans.

So roll the dice, if you dare,

and play this game to win.

We are all human, we all do sin,

never doubt yourself, never down yourself,

just believe in yourself, til the end of your days,

and know in this life

life is a game to be played.

So play to win.

Rule 2: Life is a Game to be Played

I still remember til this day what my auntie told me when I was young and going through alot. I remember she said, "I can see the future, and it looks better than it is right now." I've kept that with me through thick and thin, and that phrase has gotten me through alot in my life. So no matter what situation you might think you are in or how hard you think your situation is, there is always somebody out there doing worse, all you have to do is put one foot in front of the other and keep it moving because you can never see progress standing in one spot forever. Just put one foot in front of the other and say, "I can see the future, and it looks better than it is right now," and watch how things start to get better with time. You have to believe first in God, then believe in self, and everything else will fall into place.

In time I've learned that in order to be successful you have to have a roadmap, you have to have a plan. Nobody travels across the country without a map, otherwise they would be lost. Nobody that really wants to get to their destination will travel without a GPS, which comes in handy even if you know where you're going. My main thing is to first love God in your life and, second, have a roadmap or GPS. You have to have a plan of what you want to do. Make a plan, write down all of your goals and dreams. I mean anything you can imagine because everything is possible, as long as you put your mind to it, you can do it. Write down all your goals and dreams in the order that you want them to happen. You can put dates that you want your goals and dreams to be accomplished, and once accomplished just check them off. You will feel so much better to know that you're going in the right direction and you're making progress in your life. So remember, no matter your situation, just stand tall and say, "I can see the future, and it looks better than it looks right now."

After you get all your goals in order, you need to plan, plot, and strategize to set the world on fire. Let people know about your goals and dreams because what's an idea if nobody knows about it? Take all the polite feedback that is given to you and even the negative because we all know somebody is going to hate, but let them hate and let them add fuel to your fire as you continue to set the world on fire. While you're out chasing dreams and getting goals accomplished all your haters are lost without a roadmap to their dreams.

So be smart about what you do and do it well because nobody can do you better than you. Believe in what you do and although there are roadblocks, without them what would be so great about your story? Nobody's perfect, we all go through things in life, only the strong survive. If you have a plan, believe in your plan. If you are at McDonald's right now and you plan to be the President of the United States, you can make it with a plan. Alot of people lack ambition and I say to them, "Pray about it" because without prayer you will be a sitting duck, waiting for a handout, and in this lifetime there are no handouts.

In this life you get what you deserve, and life is not about working hard, its about working smart. You'll learn that it's not about what you know, it's about who you know. Life is as hard as you make it, you can be an entrepreneur with your own business and workers working for you, or you can work a nine-to-five for the rest of your life - clocking in and out, hating your job, taking your problems home, saying "yes, sir" and "no, sir" to somebody who doesn't respect you, or you can live your life at your pace, make money, be your own boss, and live life to the fullest because you only live once. You have to stand up for yourself and say, "I can do this," and make it happen.

It's up to you whether you want to leave a mark on this earth before you hit the exit, it's up to you if you want your haters to hate you all the way to the grave. Even if you don't have anybody or you are surrounded by the wrong people, I'm talking about people who won't you to do for them all the time, but they don't want to do for you. Remember, people won't bring you a cup of soup to keep you alive, but they will bring you flowers when you die. You have to be careful who you hang around because people will get you off track. Surround yourself with people who are upbeat and that are doing good and that are where you want to be. In this life if you find yourself a rabbit, it's like finding a pot of gold. A rabbit is a mentor, someone who is where you want to be.

Stay away from miserable people. I'm not being mean or downing anybody, but have you ever heard that misery loves company? Well if you hang around miserable people expect to live like that. Stay away from people who complain all day, stay down, and have no ambition. Stay away from hard-headed people who don't listen because they think they know it all. People like that put themselves in that position by not listening first. In order to be a leader you have to first listen and learn. So just remember, life is a game to be played, so play to win and be remembered for all the accomplishments you achieved in life.

CHAPTER 4

RULE 3
Walk by Faith, Not by Sight

Walk by Faith, Not by Sight

At times I feel lost, at times I feel trapped,

at times I feel neglected, even with a map.

My time is this moment, I have no time to waste,

so I strive hard to conquer, I always keep the faith

When my time has passed, when I'm dead and gone,

I want to be remembered, remembered that I was strong.

My gift is to lead, yes, I am a leader,

My dreams will be accomplished, my name will be remembered.

I always was a star, since the day I was born;

in my heart, I felt pain, and I'm not talking about the norm.

But with time and change

I use God as my vest,

to get through my days, to get through my nights.

In time I've learned I had to fight,

in time I learned you gotta walk by faith, not by sight.

Rule 3: Walk by Faith, Not by Sight

Do you want to be remembered? Do you want to have a legacy when you are gone from this earth? Or do you want to be that person that was alive and never lived to see their dreams come true? In order to set the world on fire, you have to put your faith in God and walk by faith, not by sight. You have to do you and follow your heart to the fullest, and never let your haters pull you down. Sometimes you might be in situations that you knew from the start you should have listened to your instincts and wouldn't be in that situation. Walking by faith is not hard to do, it's that feeling in your heart and that voice in your head that tells you the way.

You can have a plan, you can have a roadmap, but you still have to walk by faith, not by sight. If you think your plan is the greatest plan in the world, well let me tell you that is nothing because God will see you through to get you to your goals and your dreams and make them bigger than you could ever imagine. Walk by faith, not by sight is a seed that needs to be planted in your heart, mind, and soul. As long as you think of it and believe in it, it can happen.

Trust your heart, and you can go wherever your heart wants you to go. Have no fear of failure because failure, in the end, makes you stronger. In time you can do something and fail a million times, but ask yourself: "How strong was I when I started, what mind state did I have when I started, what direction was I headed when I started?" Now I'm here a million tries later, stronger and ten times farther than my eyes could see. That is why you have to walk by faith, not by sight because although you might fail sometimes, failure is a trophy. Failure can't always be looked upon as a negative because had you not failed you would have never known what it felt like to fail and you would have never learned from that situation. A man will never be a man until he has felt the pain of failure. Failure only puts the fuel to the fire, and that fire is ambition.

So whatever you can dream, don't be scared to put it to the test. There will be times when you will fail, but the goal is to never give up. You will have people tell you it won't work or you have to do this and do that. People are so negative. You can tell them about this idea, that this dream came from God, and nobody, I mean nobody, is going to stop me from making it a reality.

In order to be a successful person you have to be the master of your own mind, meaning be free and not become a slave to someone else's ideas. Believe in your dream. Although you may be working long, hard hours at a factory, believe in your dream. Although you feel down and out without a car, the key is to believe. If you believe in self, your mind will believe in you; if you believe in self, people will believe in you. If you believe and walk by faith, not by sight, God will make the rest happen for you.

CHAPTER 5

RULE 4

BELIEVE IN SELF

Believe in Me

I believe in self, trust me.

I believe til my last breath.

Believe in me when I'm down in need of help -

my dark days and dark nights be a hell of a fight.

Sometimes all I need is you to believe

to get me through the night.

I know God has my back, and He has all the love

when I need a little hug.

I put my faith in God,

I get through my trials and tribulations,

at the end I thank Him,

I praise Him that he saved me.

My time is now, and I know it;

I only live once, so I live my life to the fullest.

Cause I only live once,

if I believe in me,

I know in my heart you'll do the same.

If I fail, if I don't succeed,

then I'm the one to blame.

Rule 4: Believe in Self

Now that you have your goals and dreams on your mind, and you believe in your goals and dreams with all your heart, don't be scared to share them with the world. Believe in what God has planned for you, believe in self. Tell your friends and family about your goals and dreams. Some will lift you up, some will try to pull you down. Then you will know who to keep around.

No matter what people say, believe in your dreams and believe in self. Have self-confidence in yourself and don't let nobody stop you on your way to success. Who cares about how negative people feel about what you are doing. At the end of the day, what are they doing? Tell your family what you have in store and your plans for the future. Family will lift you up and help you on your journey.

Don't get me wrong, I know some families have issues and you have to distance yourself from them. If you feel you have to go to the other direction and turn the other cheek, follow your heart and do what you feel is right and believe in self. If you feel nobody has your back, always remember God always has your back. Good friends will gladly want to know how you feel about life and your goals and dreams, especially a good woman. A good woman is a good listener, and she will always be there to listen to what you have to say. She will be proud to know that you have an idea of where you are going, instead of just being alive without a plan and not knowing where you are going.

Some people you tell about your goals and dreams will laugh, some people will take you as a joke, but it's up to you to move forward and prove them wrong. You have to believe in self when times get hard; every day is not going to be a walk in the park, every day is not going to be pretty, but as long as you're moving forward and you're putting forth effort towards your goals and dreams, every day you're a step closer to getting them accomplished.

CHAPTER 6

RULE 5
Search for Knowledge

A Mother's Child

I gave birth to you, I gave you life.

Now just breathe and achieve,

be the best you can be in reality.

Since birth you were meant to reach your destiny;

just put your faith in God, and He'll make sure you achieve.

Believe in the things you do

cause no one on this planet earth can do the things you do.

You were blessed with a gift, knowledge is power;

search for knowledge with a vengeance, and you will devour.

Watch for snitches and fakes cause they will mislead you;

friends with no love, really don't need you.

Fight with a passion, you gotta be strong,

goals and dreams in this life are worth holding on.

Although I'm your mother, and you are my child,

there will be people who will guide you, who will make you smile.

So have faith in God when times get hard,

pray daily so you never fall apart.

The little things you know will get you through the night,

and when you wake up everything will be alright.

Rule 5: Search for knowledge

Knowledge is an eternal journey. You can never be too smart or too wise, you can only better yourself with knowledge and become wiser as you progress through life. Learn from people, life, and books. Surround yourself with good, knowledgeable people that know more than you, that way you can learn from them. Surrounding yourself with people who always look up to you will stunt your growth and will put your life and knowledge at a halt. It's alright having people look up to you, but you have to have some people that you look up to.

A mentor or a rabbit is a good person to be around, especially when it comes to a venture you want to excel in and become great. I believe that everyone is born a leader, but it is up to you to be an intelligent follower in order to become a great leader. Life in general will prepare you in the future for future events; things you didn't know then has prepared you for the now. It's all about knowledge. If nobody paid any attention to others and through life with their eyes and ears shut, who would be the leaders of tomorrow? The leaders of the past even had to search for knowledge in order to get ideas to become great leaders. Check out how the pyramids were built, check out how the light bulb was invented, check out how Barack Obama became the first African-American President. All of them had something in common - they all had to search for knowledge in order to have great ideas, to become great leaders.

Life is a game to be played, so play to win, and you will win by obtaining knowledge in order to survive. Books are great tools for obtaining knowledge. The library is your friend, and it will show you the way. When I was younger I used to hate reading books, not because I hated books in general, but because the schools forced me to read books I couldn't relate to. I think teachers should be prohibited from making kids read books that don't pertain to them and giving them an "F" for effort. When in reality had you given that child something they could relate to, that child would have made an "A+." If teachers would be more truthful about what's really going on in the world, more leaders would rise at an earlier age, instead of them waiting for that child to grow and learn the difference between a good, knowledgeable book and a book that doesn't mean anything.

Everybody is born with a clean slate. It is up to you to live and learn what's real and what's fake; it is up to you what you put into your mind, body, and soul; it's up to you. Knowledge is power, believe that with your heart, then follow your heart, and your heart is God's heart so He will send you to your next destination. When people say, "Books are boring and they put me to sleep," ask them what books they are reading, what are the titles, what are the morals of the books, did the cover look good, did you read the back, or did you read the table of contents? Don't get me wrong, all books aren't meant for all people, just like all movies aren't meant for all people. Some you will like, and some you won't. It's up to you to choose which one fits you.

CHAPTER 7

RULE 6
Stop Procrastinating, Stop Worrying

God's Hands

I've never felt this way before. A feeling like I'm bout to jump off a cliff and be caught by the hands of God. I never felt like this before. Like I'm bout to jump off the highest building in the world and be caught by the hands of God. My heart and mind tells me everything will be alright, just go, and He will show me the way, just trust and believe, you may not can see, but God sees and knows best. Just stay focused and follow your plan and put your life in God's hands.

Rule 6: Stop Procrastinating, Stop Worrying

Procrastination and worry is like a disease, a sickness that stops you from achieving your goals and dreams. Believe in God, put Him first, and make whatever you have planned happen. Every goal and every dream is not going to be easy to accomplish, no temple or creation was created in one day; that is something to remember as you start to procrastinate or worry. Nobody is perfect, everybody has flaws, but everybody can have a sense of direction, as long as they have a plan and follow their heart.

There are ways to get around procrastination and worry. Find all of your skills and work on one at a time, and once you get tired of working on one, switch to the other and time will tell you the truth about yourself. You will feel better about yourself once your work is done.

Are you at a stage in your life where y ou don't know who you are, or you don't know what to do? Start working on your set of skills that God has instilled in you and see the blessings and the gifts that He has for you at the end. Nobody can think like you, remember that..think about that for a moment...nobody can think like you...say it out loud...nobody can think like me, nobody can think like me, nobody can think like me. There are no two things in life that are the same. Nobody can do what another individual can do. There will never be another Michael Jordan or Michael Jackson because God created them to be them and nobody will ever be able to duplicate them, ever. So strive hard and go hard and try hard to become the person that God has made, and the only person that can do that is you.

Have a vision on what you want to do; if you don't have one, well that means you need to bow down and let God in your life and let Him show you the way. Remember that you were born on a certain time and date and will die on a certain time and date, so it matters what you do in between that time that makes you a great person or a nobody. Do you want to be remembered, or do you want to be a nobody that nobody will ever know existed? On your tombstone they will have your date of birth, a dash, and your date of death. It only matters what you do on the dash because that is what will make you great or what will make you a regular person. Funerals are only sad when you know that person never got the chance to love and be great. You have the chance now, a chance that some people will never have, so be grateful that you are alive and well and are able to move forward because every day you wake up is a blessing from God.

So stop procrastinating and worrying, and remember when nobody is there God is always there to comfort you and show you the way.

I read Dale Carnegie's book, "How to Stop Worrying and Start Living," and I feel that God showed me the way through that book. I followed my heart, and it led me to that book. One day I was just driving, true story, looking for video games, and my heart said to just go to the thrift store because you might find something that will change your life forever. And believe me, I did, and my heart led me right to this book. I was at a point in my life where I was fed up with just being alive and not living. God is your solution when you are in need and you have nobody to go to. People don't always have the answers, but God always has the right answers, and you can believe that. So with that said if you are in a place in your life and you are feeling down and out, here is a blessing from me to help lift you up and take some of your worries away.

CHAPTER 8

RULE 7
Stay Consistent and Persistent

God's Hands II

If it is to be,

then I will be.

If it is to see,

then I will see.

I put my faith in God,

I will always put Him first;

no matter the weather,

He will always be first.

Til I see my destiny

and fulfill my prophecy,

I will trust and believe

because I know the Lord is inside me.

My heart is of gold,

my soul is of diamonds,

I'm a diamond in the rough,

the Lord has found me.

The Lord will bless me,

the Lord will guide me,

yes, He will see me through.

So when you try to kick me, when I'm down,

and you don't help me through, just remember:

I'm God's son, and He will always be there

to see His son through.

Rule 7: Stay Consistent and Persistent

By staying consistent and persistent you will see your goals and dreams come true and become a reality before your eyes. By not being consistent and persistent with your time, it will take you longer to achieve, and there is no time to waste while alive because tomorrow is not promised. It's a good thing to keep track of what you do with your skills that God has given you, in order to keep you focused on your dreams because it is so easy to get sidetracked. Everybody gets sidetracked from time to time, but smart people who keep up with their skills day to day and apply them day to day will prosper faster.

Only time will tell how passionate you are about what you are doing because if you are passionate about what you are doing, your work becomes your play and every day you wake up with a smile on your face because you're not waking up to go to work, you're waking up to go play.

Have you heard of the matrix, sure you have; have you heard of haters, sure you have; have you ever had somebody say what you can't do, sure you have. Well let me tell you about something I call the matrix. If you stay consistent and persistent, nine times out of ten your haters are to busy worrying about what you are doing, therefore, time passes them by as you progress through time, and they become lost in time. By the next time you see them, you have become a better person, a better man or woman. You are no longer wearing non-namebrand, you are wearing Roc-a-wear or Sean John; you are no longer riding in a broken down car that breaks down every week and you have to depend on someone to pick you up, you are flossin in a Benz, a Bentley, or Bugatti or whatever you put your mind on.

My whole thing about the matrix is zone into yourself, find yourself, do you, and the next time you see someone that you know that doesn't want you to succeed, watch the look on their face. I guarantee it will be a sick look like, "I can't believe this, how could this be, this is impossible." But the only thing that is impossible is nothing, and you can believe that.

Hustlers don't sleep, hustlers wake up with the sun and stay up with the night. Hustlers dream only for a second because hustlers are so in touch with reality. Hustlers don't sleep because while you sleep you become a sheep and in order to be a hustler you have to be a wolf. So next time you sleep, remember you are the sheep. Hustlers don't sleep, hustlers pray and say to God, "Show me the way."

Remember, life is a game, so play to win; life is a game, play to win. Just like a video game you play to win, you stay consistent and persistent until you win. If you apply that same attitude towards life, you will become a great leader, you will find yourself and find self and become so self-confident that the greatest of all leaders will praise you for what you have accomplished.

CHAPTER 9

RULE 8
Never be Scared of Change

747

Today I saw the numbers "747" flash on my phone.

Today I got the message I should go back home.

Just like a 747 going to heaven,

things are bound to change.

If I stay in this position,

then I'm the one to blame.

I just wanna be free,

I just wanna be me,

I just wanna be somebody.

So I will take a leap of faith

and land in God's hands

cause I know in my heart

He understands my plans.

So just like a 747 going to heaven,

I wanna fly away

cause I know tomorrow

brings me a better day.

Rule 8: Never be Scared of Change

I come from sweet home Alabama, and I'm proud of it. I learned alot while there, although once I moved to Nashville it opened my eyes wider. While I was in Alabama I noticed something about the people that was around me. It was like they were scared of positive change. They would rather go to work and be a slave in a factory for chump change, than try to get an education or use their minds and save up for a business that they could run themselves. I'm not knocking anybody, I'm just saying there are alot of people out there that they know they could be doing better, but the question is do you want to be better, do you want to change.

I will never talk down on anybody, but never go through life expecting a handout because it won't happen. You have to get off your behind, put one foot in front of the other, and make it happen. If you are scared of change, pray about it, God will show you the way and make you a better person in the process. Never be scared of change, if you are scared of change you are scared to live because you can be alive, but the question is are you living.

I come from a small city called Florence, Alabama, and the people who actually make it out don't come back, only for holidays maybe. That's because where you come from you gotta get away in order to live. If you stay it's like a trap, you will end up in a factory, depressed with no money.   There is one club, and after awhile you see everybody that you went to school with, so the club is nothing. Even when you get out and you go back, if you go to the club it's more like a reunion. People have more respect for you that you made it out and that you are successful.

I know there are people that love where they are from and can't wait to go back home. Don't get me wrong, I love my city with all my heart, but it doesn't make me happy to stay there or go back often because i'm a person that wants to live, not just be alive and die and not be remembered. I'm a man that's never been scared of change because in order to grow you have to change and move forward in life.

I dedicate this chapter to my city and to all the people who know me and the people who want to know me. Never be scared of change, never be scared to become a great leader instead of an intelligent follower. Put faith in God and let Him show you the way to a better life and a brighter future. Where I'm from, either you make it out or you die, and I'm not talking about death itself by a gun, I'm taking about your goals and dreams, your mindstate, your ability to live.

So, with that being said, I know some people with kids and people doing time, etc. That's life, tomorrow is a new day, and you can either change for the better or for the worse. You either can slave in a factory for the rest of your life and hate your job for the rest of your life, or you can make a better way for you and your kids by using your brain, instead of your hands. Remember, "a mind is a terrible thing to waste."

If you are locked up and doing time, do the time, don't let the time do you. If they have a library, focus on making yourself a better person, and by the time you're done with your time, you've become a better person, a better man or woman, people will respect you more, and you can teach people or show people a better way.

So, remember, at the end of the day, your life is in God's hands, and He will show you the way. Change is good. Dreams are a mile away, but goals will be accomplished as your heart shows you the way. Only you can make it happen. Never be scared of change. If you sit and let time pass you by, then you are the one to blame. Never be scared of change.

CHAPTER 10

RULE 9
Stay Alive

Last Day on Earth

If this is my last day on the earth,

I will treat my niggaz with respect.

If this is my last day on this earth,

I would hug my mother and father

and tell them I love them.

If this is my last day on this earth,

I would hug my sisters in the physical form

and tell them I love them even more.

If this is my last day on this earth,

I would pray for my enemies

and still wish them well.

If this is my last day on this earth.

Rule 9: Stay Alive

There are alot of successful people who are miserable and unhappy. Their goals and dreams are being accomplished, they have money, cars, clothes, and maybe someone to love, but, at the end of the day, you have to love yourself before you can love someone else. You have to know who you are before you can get to know someone else. you have to know what keeps you alive and sane in order to be happy in life because you can have a billion people who love you, but if you don't love you, all that love from other people doesn't matter. All the cars, houses, fans, shoes, etc. doesn't matter, you have to find out who you are in order to be truly happy with self, and in order to do that you have to stay alive!

If you put a .45cal to your head or overdose on drugs, you will never know the person that God has made, only He will know. It's up to you to stay alive and live life to the fullest, to find out the person you are. Trust me, there will be many roadblocks and many traps, but it is up to you to surpass them and keep reaching for the stars. Nobody can by you, nobody can breathe the air you breathe but you. I alway say, "Life is a game, so play to win," but you can't win if you blow your brains out.

Nothing feels better than success. Everybody goes through trials and tribulations, and nobody will ever be perfect. There will be people that will hate you for what you do. I know that there will be people that will hate me for writing this book, but do I care, of course not. I will tell them it was God's will that led me to express myself through this book, to reach out to kids and adults, to try to help them with their lives because everybody doesn't have guidance, everybody wasn't born with a silver spoon in their mouths, every kid doesn't have a mother or father that's a teacher, doctor, or lawyer, every kid doesn't get the proper training. So with this book I will do my best to reach them and to teach them and show them a better way through life.

So I will stay alive! When times are hard, stay alive! When your haters say give up, stay alive! Because tomorrow is a new day, and God has a guaranteed gift for you when you wake up, and that gift is life. So stay alive!

CHAPTER 11

RULE 10
Respect All, but Fear None

The Appreciation (2014)

People who don't appreciate your presence
will not be there to bury you.
People who don't appreciate you're gonna
die at midnight, don't appreciate your presence.
People who hold grudges and don't forgive,
don't appreciate your presence.
People who don't respect themselves, so they don't respect you,
so how could they respect your presence?
People you don't love
will not appreciate your presence.
People who don't want to be around you
will not appreciate your presence.
People who don't want to see you access greater heights
will not appreciate your presence.
So the question is "why be around people
who don't appreciate your presence?"
Be around people
who appreciate your presence.

Rule 10: Respect All, but Fear None

Be a leader, but protect yourself by any means necessary, and I mean that with all my heart. People will try you, people will test you just to see if you stand for what you believe in. People never want to see another surpass them in life, people are like crabs: once they see you trying to get out of the situation that you are in, they will try to pull you back down. Trust nobody, believe in self and God, and keep it moving, no matter what situation you think you are in; as long as you are moving you will see the other side.

Be careful who you disrespect because he or she could come back to you. People tend to hold grudges and hold on to them til the grave. Be careful of the people you insult because that might be the door to your success, and you should never judge someone til you get to know someone. I know you've heard the term "burn bridges," so no matter how mad someone might make you, sometimes it's best to accept that criticism and keep it as a life lesson and turn it into a positive.

Respect all, fear none. Keep this with you while on your journey. Keep your head up, stay positive, and keep it moving.

As you get bigger and get money in your pockets, there will be people watching. Yes, those same people who laughed at you when you were broke will be the same people that will try to take you for everything you've worked for. It can be your family or friends. It's more than likely to be family because they are the closest ones to you, so be careful and keep your eyes open for your enemies.

If you don't have haters, you are doing something wrong, so get to moving and get some. Remember, the same people who wouldn't bring you a bowl of soup to keep you alive will be at your funeral when you die. The same people who didn't come to your birthday party or call to see if you were alive will be at your funeral when you die. So my inspiration for living and getting my goals and dreams accomplished is making sure that my funeral is the baddest and the most untouchable funeral ever remembered in the hearts, minds, and souls of mankind; not only for my haters, not only for my enemies, but also for the people who loved me and cherished my every moment on the planet earth. Because while I was here I know I only had one life to live, one direction to go, and one gate to enter.

So as I hit the exit, remember you only have one life to live, one direction to go, and one gate to enter. Live life to the fullest, be remembered for your accomplishments. Respect all, fear none. Put your faith in God and stay **B.L.A.C.**, a **B**orn **L**eader **A**ccepting **C**riticism, under the sun, til the day God calls you home. So it's forever **B.L.A.C. NATION**, one nation under God til I die, don't cry, I'm more happy in the sky.

CHAPTER 12

B.L.A.C. POETRY

Red & Black Roses

Give me roses while I'm alive,

give me roses to smell, before I die.

Give me my red roses, my red roses,

so I know your love's no lie.

Give me my red roses, my red roses, before I die,

give me my red roses, under the sun in the sky.

Give me a dozen red roses, while I'm alive,

give me my red roses before I die.

If it's too late for you to give me my red roses,

there's always black roses.

The ones from the haters that hate,

The ones that breed envy and hate.

The ones that cause heartache,

The ones that's too late.

FUCK Y'ALL!

You never loved me in the first place!

I wear my black roses, just like my red roses,

on my sleeves to bring my haters to their knees.

To let them know that I breathe success,

you see, it's just a reminder of success.

That people envy and love,

that people love and hate,

either or, it's ok, it's just a figure of speech.

And trust is always an issue,

whether you or me.

So just remember while I was alive you didn't bring me a cup of soup,

to keep me alive, so why bring me red roses when I die?

While I was alive I said I was sorry,

but you still never forgave, you still tortured.

So there was no forgiveness for sorry,

so over time I still paid.

So why bring me red roses when I die?

If you have the balls to see a born leader buried,

if you have the balls to come to the funeral,

bring me black roses.

Let people know, while I was alive you didn't care,

let people know that you kicked me when I was down.

Let people know you didn't want me with my crown,

let them know!

Let them know these pussy niggaz put me in the ground,

let them know!

Before you put black roses on top of my casket in the ground,

let them know before they put dirt on my roses and I'm six feet underground.

That I was one of the realest motherfuckers that stood tall above ground.

Bridges

If the shoe was on the other foot

I wouldn't do what you do simply because you burn bridges.

Bridges that can make you a better person,

bridges that can change your life forever.

Instead of running to a problem, you ran from a problem,

instead of facing a problem, you destroy what's already built.

You can run in life, but you can't run forever.

You can cry in life, but you can't cry forever.

Life will continue to go, and the world will continue to turn,

so be careful of the bridges you burn.

Just because you lose trust in someone

doesn't mean you can't forgive and move forward.

Just because someone makes you cry or has issues in their life that you don't approve

doesn't mean put them out your life.

When an apology is given, and a sorry is accepted,

it's suppose to be a new beginning, a bond that can be made stronger.

So be careful of the bridges you burn,

by forgiving and acting like the person you just accepted the apology from don't exist.

It's not the right thing to do, it's actually torture,

if there's love involved and you care about that person, would you want it done to you?

So be careful of the bridges you burn.

There are only so many people in life with roadmaps, GPS, and walk by faith in God.

I'm one of them.

So be careful of the bridges you burn.

So being the man I am I won't let you burn this one.

I will guide you to success because I know your heart, and we all make mistakes.

Love after Love

Maybe one day I will see my love,

my love that comes after love.

The one that God has prepared for me,

the one that I will adore.

If I am an angel of God,

then He shall send me an angel worth waiting for.

An angel with wings so warm

she can stop a heart from being cold.

We will fly high in the sky with wings of steel,

we both will achieve, no one will stop us as we proceed to be free.

I will protect her from harm, with my heart so pure,

trust will not be the norm.

I'm the one she will trust in time of need,

I'm the one she comes to for whatever she needs.

Only we as on will conquer the world together,

so it's us against the world, may our love last forever...love after love.

Only God can Hear Me

Staring at the world, as my heart years for peace,

while asking my Heavenly Father why they judge me.

Cursed within, with a drop of sin,

and since I'm not dipped, I'll never get out this pen.

They say I'm bound for hell to live eternal life,

but what If I wanna get baptized by Jesus Christ?

I know one day I'll walk five steps to the hands of God's Son,

and He'll tell me to hold my breath

as He washes my body from sin, to put me closer to death.

So tell me, if I never get dipped, will you still love me?

Probably not, you go to church every Sunday, and you still judge me.

To all of you hypocrites, that's full of shit, trying to kill my dreams,

so quick to judge, but y'all scared to get y'all hands clean.

Let the preacher say another prayer for me, just in case God ignores me,

since I'm not baptized, I think the devil's looking for me.

My eyes teary, now who hears me, who fears me,

who will walk behind this leader screaming, "Only God can hear me"?

Ready to Die

I'm on a mission to find Jesus Christ.

Hopefully He won't try to resurrect my life.

To see the dead could end so much pain,

and I know He's the one Who can take my pain.

Reality is so truthfully inspired by death,

it's been a long way coming while praying for help.

Teardrops hit the roots of the cycle of life,

let it burn til this cold world turns it to ice.

Let the rain pour down til it clears my mind,

While I'm stuck in the mist, trying to put the past behind.

I'm on a suicidal mission, I'm trapped in a position

where my family and friends don't want to listen.

So I grab my pen and paper to find a better way to make it,

at least my paper won't talk back, even though I fell off the map.

It'll never down me, never leave me feeling trapped;

it'll always be there, to have my back.

Fuck a bitch, never there, never will be,

never will be in a four-corner room to heal me.

So feel me when you fucked up,

nigga, when you finally grown up,

you find out your fake friends, and bitch never show up.

Let it Burn

No need to hold it up inside,

let your soul cry, to let the world know what's inside.

AS your flesh burns and yearns, as you start to quiver,

teardrops fall, as your body starts to shiver.

Fuck the world, let 'em feel your pain,

They ain't lived it, so it drives them insane.

They don't know shit that God put you through,

it's more or less the stress, chill bumps on your flesh.

Until it's your turn to die, live and learn,

until you see the pearly gates, let this motherfucker burn.

I know you feel it as your heart feels helpless

ready for whatever, no need to feel selfish.

Baptize yourself in your own tears, drown your fears,

as the faded memories come back.

While you think about the good times as you rewind,

wishing they would come back,

wondering if you'll ever see your loved ones again.

Holla if you hear me, pour out a little liquor,

burning like a shot of country boy liquor.

Waiting patiently for God to come back to heal you,

let the world feel you.

Let the rage fade away,

by tomorrow everything will be ok.

Backbone

Dear mom and pops:

I thank you for what you did or done

cause without you I wouldn't see the sun rise.

I'm not surprised by what you both done for me,

When I'm down and out I remember you both love me.

Born 05/31/86 from the bricks to suburbs

which had alot of unions blurred.

We still struggle, like no other,

it's just we rely on one another

to be strong and forever hold on.

Bred to have the heart of a lion,

and never to be defined

and take on the world as if the world were mine.

Even when things get complicated

I don't pick up the chrome, I pick up the phone.

So where would I be without my backbone?

Rebel Flags

Rebel flags everywhere,

it ain't disappeared through the years.

Your fears in your kids,

the past makes the future.

So we live in the moment, while we grow to see,

things change by the moment.

We fight for justice, beg for freedom by the night,

while our dreams are crushed by rebel flags at night.

It only complicates the future inside our communities,

when deep inside we know all it takes is unity.

Get Away aka My Wings

Give me my wings so I can fly in the sky to my dreams,

Give me the knowledge so I can give back to my seeds.

Let them breathe and find a better way for tomorrow,

hopefully, they can see through the pain and the sorrow.

Lord, forgive them for the things they don't know,

watch over them from heaven, make sure my seeds grow.

Trials and tribulations, I'm sure they will come,

make sure they stand firm as a leader, and never run.

Time will show who can stand the tests of time,

make sure they follow leaders cause blind can't lead blind.

The only way to lead and succeed, you gotta listen,

so listen to your peers, and your seeds will pay attention.

Search for knowledge, knowledge is the way to success, do you feel blessed?

Life is a game, nothing but a game to be played,

maybe one day you'll get your wings and fly away.

Colorblind

If people see what I see they would see a queen,

a queen with a heart that is pure and sweet.

If people see what I see they would see, not just a woman,

but a phenomenal woman with the mind that could change the world, hcal the blind.

If people see what I see they would see an everlasting friend.

If people see what I see they would not see color,

they would see a beautiful woman with ambition and love that could cure heartache.

A queen, that's what I see.

If people see what I see they wouldn't see color, nor would they be blind,

but when they see you they would know your heart is good and would be colorblind.

27 Roses

If I gave you roses they would die in a couple of days.

If I gave you candy it would make your belly ache.

If I gave you a stuffed animal you would love it for a day,

then in a year you would throw it away.

If I gave you perfume you would smell good,

but your natural scent smells better.

If I gave you a card you would read it, you would love it,

but it was not directly from my heart.

So I give you 27 roses, straight poetry from my heart,

from mine to yours.

When it rains, my heart is yours;

when it pours, my heart is yours;

when you're scared, I'm there;

when you're down, I care;

this is not just a poem.

27 roses is 27 years,

from my heart to your heart.

What makes this the best gift ever

is that through this poem and through you, I will live forever.

Millions without Love

I see me counting money on the kitchen floor,

throwing money high, til it hits the floor.

Counting money til it ain't no more,

but it means nothing without you.

Taking trips around the globe, new houses, talking marble floors,

Maybach's and Ferrari doors,

but it means nothing without you.

I know I might have lost your trust,

that's why it seems like there's no us.

No communication means no us,

that's why I gotta find my way back to you.

What's a million dollars without love,

what's a relationship without trust,

what's a future without us,

what's a million dollars without love?

Throwing money at Niagara Falls,

smoking on loud while the water falls,

but it means nothing without you.

Taking funny pictures with fans,

everybody thinking I'm the man,

but inside I'm a lonely man.

Somethings people don't understand,

nothings is the same without you.

Riding down Sunset Boulevard,

in a Phantom, its a nice car,

plushed out, going hard,

but it would mean nothing without you.

So what's a million dollars without love,

what's a relationship without trust,

what's a future without us,

what's a million dollars without love?

Role Model to a Child

How can I be a role model to a child

when the odds are against me?

I smoke, I drink my pain away

so I don't feel no pain,

I smoke, I drink just to stay sane.

How can I be a role model to a child?

I chill with my niggaz,

smoke with my niggaz,

wild out with my niggaz.

So how can I be a role model to a child?

I love women and fuck with the bitches

and love hanging with them, at least some times.

How can I be a role model to a child

when I run the streets, hustle in the streets, bang in the streets?

Shit, a nigga gotta eat, shit this child gotta eat.

How can I be a role model to a child

when I drink and turn up, damn near an alcoholic?

So in your eyes you see me failing,

How can I be a role model to a child

when I smoke blunt after blunt, joint after joint, and get so high

I swear I'm at the gates of heaven?

How can I be a role model to a child?

How can I be?

Change......................

If One Man Could Change the World

If one man could change the world, would you believe in him, if he believed in himself? Would you follow him and believe in his heart and courage to pull you through your hard times and tribulations? If you believe in him then you should believe in yourself because we are all one and born leaders til our last breath. Two minds are more powerful than one, and a nation is stronger than two. So with these rules I give to you as a blessing to you. May my poetry go to your hearts, and through your veins may we change the world so we all live forever and the world know our names. There's a leader inside you.

Arcardio Morrez Harder., aka Caraveggio the Prince

The End